MIRACLES OF HOPE

Valerie's Journey

VALERIE ALEXANDER

Copyright © 2024 by Valerie Alexander.

ISBN: 9798890905543 (sc)
ISBN: 9798890905550 (e)

All rights reserved. No part of this book may be reproduced or transmitted in any form or by any means, electronic or mechanical, including photocopying, recording, or by any information storage and retrieval system, without permission in writing from the copyright owner.

The views expressed in this work are solely those of the author and do not necessarily reflect the views of the publisher, and the publisher hereby disclaims any responsibility for them.

EXPRESSO
Executive Center 777, Dunsmuir Street Vancouver, BC V71K4
1-888-721-0662 ext 101
info@expressopublishing.com

CONTENTS

Preface.. ix
Acknowledgements xi

The Unexpected... Expectant...Miracle.........
    Twenty Years Later........................... 1
Is It A Puzzle? 3
The Ride...The Water... The Letter... 4
The Vision.. 6
It Won't Be Long 8
The Car Accident... 9
Out of Tragedy... Comes Triumph... 13
She's My Best Friend.................................... 15
A New Life 18
The Tornado 22
Pinnacle Mountain...................................... 26
A Quiet Place.. 29
The Valley of The Shadow... of Death... 34
Daughter's Words....................................... 37
The Christmas Miracle.................................. 38
Like Pools of Blue Water............................... 41
From Hell to Heaven 43
Unforgetable 47

To my beautiful daughters
   Whose grace and strength
      Inspired my walk with Jesus

PREFACE

When my youngest daughter was eight years old, and my oldest was twenty-one, there was a snapshot of us taken. It was this candid shot that began the inspiration for this book. I decided to frame it as a black and white, to give as a Christmas gift. Today, seven years later, I find myself looking at this photo, reading the inscription I wrote on the matting surrounding the print.

Valerie and her two daughters

>Throughout history and a lifetime
>Reaching to heights far above our imaginings
>God's love is eternal
>Forever spanning yet beyond the sands of time
>God's miracle of hope
>Is Jesus

For a long time, I thought about writing a book. I never thought it would come to pass. Well…I guess…I don't think of myself as a writer. I sing. I've been singing since I was a little girl. Over the course of my life, God's blessings came in the form of miracles.

Miracles happened, in my professional and personal life. Miracles that tell a story, the story of a journey, my journey. It's become a journey of faith…a journey of prayer…and a journey of hope. It was His answers to prayer in miraculous ways that encouraged me to write this book. God has spoken to my heart, confirming that it is His hand…His grace…and His leading that…paved the way. I ask the Lord for His help in writing.

Dear Jesus,

I write this book for you, oh Lord. May it be pleasing in your sight. May God use the words on the pages that follow for His glory.

ACKNOWLEDGEMENTS

To my everlasting friend Jesus whom I acknowledge the true inspiration for the writing of "Miracles of Hope", I give Him thanks and praise for the miracles.

To my daughters, grandchildren, parents, and siblings for their love, support, smiles and laughter. May God richly bless you in your endeavors for Christ.

To my friends Larry and Arlene for lending an ear, a shoulder and helping me every step of the way. I thank you for your prayers.

To my brother John for his gifts of time, prayer and finances provided as the book was born.

May God grant you His peace and fill you with His presence. I pray for you. I love you.

THE UNEXPECTED...
EXPECTANT...MIRACLE.........
TWENTY YEARS LATER

I was born and raised in a Christian home. Although, when I think back, a lot of my childhood years were filled with strife. Some strife I caused myself. Some, I call life. Through it all, I have come to know the Lord of hope...the miracle of hope...Jesus.

As I grew in the church and my faith, God allowed me to meet a man. I should say, a boy. We were kids, eighteen, just out of high school. Three months after graduation from high school, I became pregnant with my oldest daughter.

I thought at the time it was the end of the world. But through it all my grandparents, parents, and my whole family supported me. They lifted me in prayer. I made it through the pregnancy, birth, and learned how to care for my daughter. I thank God for my parents. Both of them helped raise her during early childhood years.

Eventually, I moved out of my parents' home and got married. The decision to marry (the father of my daughter) was less than fortunate. We were both too young for the marriage commitment.

My mother-in-law was a Jehovah's Witness. It had the opportunity of witnessing to her the good news of Jesus Christ. She was enslaved in the Jehovah's Witness faith, and couldn't understand the things of God. Her eyes were not open.

I continued to pray for her for many years. About the same time the snapshot (family picture) was taken (twenty years later), she called with good news. She said she hadn't forgotten the talks we had about God. I will never forget the day she called and said she had become a Christian. She thanked me for my prayers. I can remember praying for her some mornings, as I would drive to work.

Over a period of twenty years, I recall her name coming to mind. I know now it was Christ nudging me to lift her in prayer. The Lord spoke to my heart and I prayed…many times in tongues… for her. I believe it was Him allowing her to find Christ through the means of intercessory prayer. She came to know the Lord of hope… Jesus… through the power of the Holy Spirit in prayer.

Eventually her son and I parted ways. We were too young for the marriage commitment. The relationship, I knew the day we married…wasn't right. I married him out of the fear of being alone.

A single mom, I moved back home with my parents. They helped me. Still not sure of my future, I enrolled in college. In a small town nearby, I started on the path to becoming a nurse.

IS IT A PUZZLE?

I felt lonely much of the time, after my divorce. I think it was about this time I began to search…to search for God. On my knees, at times, I prayed. I asked the Lord to help me find the purpose and meaning of my life.

Looking back, I call it a puzzle. My life was like a puzzle, and I was in search of that missing piece. I tried and tried to find it. I wasn't sure where I would find it, or what I would do to find it. But I knew…that someone…or something was missing.

Having some experiences with God as I grew up, I knew I was saved. When I was in the sixth grade I attended a winter bible camp. During my camp experience, God gave me the gift of speaking in tongues.

I used the gift I had in personal prayer. Many hours of prayer were spent praying for other people. Many hours were spent looking… searching for that missing puzzle piece.

THE RIDE...THE WATER...
THE LETTER...

I got involved in a relationship during my nursing career that was...kind of rocky...but I loved him. We had our share of ups and downs; and we had a lot of fun together. It was a few years later when our relationship broke up. That breakup left me heartbroken... crushed. I felt hopeless. Life for me had lost its meaning.

Shortly after nursing graduation, I drove to a nearby state with a friend. We were going to a party to celebrate. The drive was approximately one hour. We drove along a winding road heading north. We were on our way to a bar to have some drinks.

The read was treacherous, filled with S curves, steep hills, drop offs, and cliffs. Some of the cliffs were without guardrails, next to a river bed. The road took us next to curves and drop offs that were dangerously close to the water.

At the tavern we had a few too many. I was the designated driver...since I was more sober than she. I couldn't stand up.

We sat for another hour. I quit drinking alcohol and started on coffee. She continued her drinking binge. I carried her to the car. I was in no shape to drive. But...I did.

I remember on the way home waking up while the car was in motion. I was headed straight for the water until something woke me up and turned the wheel. I vaguely remember the drive home.

I woke up the next day in bed fully clothed. It was late in the afternoon. I wondered how I got there...and when. My heart trembled as I realized the only thing I could remember was the wheel being turned and seeing the water coming at me.

How did I get home? Did I drop my friend off and where? I remember getting on my knees, asking God for help…to never again drink to the point of excess (to the point that I couldn't remember).

I walked out to my car. As I walked, my body literally shook. I searched every inch of my car for a dent, hoping that I had not gotten into an accident or hurt someone. I was relieved to find that my vehicle was unharmed…and I was safe.

About this time I went to bed one night…and had a dream. I talked to my grandmother about the dream. I explained it to her. She interpreted my dream…and told me. It wasn't a dream. It was a vision.

THE VISION

It was a dream I had three nights in a row. I didn't want to go to sleep...I was afraid. Would I dream it again?

In my vision I was standing in the middle of a blacktop road in the country. It was night time. The moon was bright. The sky was clear. There were no street lights. The moon was bright enough to illuminate the surrounding landscape.

There were cornfields on both sides of the road and ditches... kind of like the Illinois prairie. I was walking down the center of the road...following painted lines. Then I heard a noise to my right.

I looked over and saw only cornfields. But I couldn't resist. What was the noise? I started toward the field. I went through the ditch, climbed over the fence...and walked through the cornfields toward the sound.

It was...as if it really happened. I could smell the corn. I could feel the corn blades slapping me in the arms and face as I walked through the corn rows. Then I came upon a clearing.

In the clearing everyone was there that was important to me (family and friends). They were chattering and conversing. Suddenly there was a loud noise. The ground started to shake. It was...as if there was an earthquake. People were running and screaming.

Then I saw a hand. It was huge. (Remember the commercials for insurance where the hand held up the world globe). The hand came down from the sky, all the way to the earth. People got in line. One by one I watched as they stepped onto his hand. Then He lifted them up.

I remember being the last one in line. I put one foot in His hand and had one foot on the ground. He started to lift His hand. It was then I woke up. I never know. I never knew if I made it.

The third night I experienced this dream I didn't wake up like I had before. I was covered in sweat with the sheet wrapped around my body. I realized then I had jumped and bolted in front of the footboard, standing straight on my feet. The first thought that hit my brain: What was my purpose in life…and why was I here?

IT WON'T BE LONG

Shortly after having the dream, I received a letter in the mail from my aunt. She wrote the lyrics to a song that played over and over in my head. It was about how we don't have much time here on this earth and about the fact that someday Jesus would return. She wrote how I had to search for my purpose in life…and that my purpose was in Christ.

Here are some of the song lyrics that were written in that letter…

> It won't be long
> 'Til we'll be leaving here
> It won't be long
> We'll be going home
>
> Count the years as months
> Count the months as weeks
> Count the weeks as days
> We'll be going home

THE CAR ACCIDENT...

In my prayers today I hear one thing. God speaking to my heart... saying... "I know what your greatest fear is...the fear of the unknown." I wasn't quite sure what that meant. I thought about it today. I continued to pray He would reveal what it was supposed to mean for me. Eventually He spoke to my heart saying, "I am the God of the unknown...and the known."

I always hoped to reconcile the things of my past that were painful and unknown. One of the greatest things I wondered about... was a relationship problem with my mother. I wondered why we had difficulty getting along and also about the problems we had in our relationship. I also wondered why we had gotten into a tragic car accident when I was three years old...and my sister was five.

Two passages of scripture come to mind (especially for this chapter).

(Romans 8:28 NKJV) And we know that all things work together for good to those who love God, to those who are called according to His purpose.

Another passage of scripture involves Thomas, one of Jesus' disciples. It's about the disbelief of Thomas, in regards to the appearance of Jesus in the upper room after the resurrection of Christ.

(John 20:19-29 NKJV) 19 Then, the same day at evening, being the first day of the week, when the doors were shut

where the disciples were assembled, for fear of the Jews, Jesus came and stood in the midst, and said to them, "Peace be with you!" 20 When He had said this, He showed them His hands and His side. Then the disciples were glad when they saw the Lord. 21 So Jesus said to them again, "Peace to you! As the Father has sent Me, I also send you." 22 And when He had said this, He breathed on them, and said to them, "Receive the Holy Spirit. 23 If you forgive the sins of any, they are forgiven them; if you retain the sins of any, they are retained." 24 Now Thomas, called the Twin, one of the twelve, was not with them when Jesus came. 25 The other disciples therefore said to him, "We have seen the Lord." So he said to them, "Unless I see in His hands the print of the nails, and put my finger into the print of the nails, and put my hand into His side, I will not believe." 26 And after eight days His disciples were again inside, and Thomas with them. Jesus came, the doors being shut, and stood in the midst, and said, "Peace to you!" 27 Then He said to Thomas, "Reach your finger here, and look at My hands; and reach your hand here, and put it into My side. Do not be unbelieving, but believing." 28 And Thomas answered and said to Him, "My Lord and my God!" 29 Jesus said to him, "Thomas because you have seen Me, you have believed. Blessed are those who have not seen and yet have believed."

As I go through struggles and trials, I remember reading that verse. I put it to memory. Sometimes I would go to my Dad for advice. At times, God would speak through him and quote that passage of scripture to me (Romans 8:28). This morning I am in prayer for this chapter.

Lord, how should this chapter unfold? What is it you would have me to say? Help me today as I write this chapter. Help me to find the answers...or some meaning to the wondering that I have... the questions.

I am reminded once again of my search for purpose in life and also my disbelief...kind of like Thomas. I think of how similar Thomas's disbelief and my own are related. There are times I can be as doubting as Thomas.

As this chapter unfolds I am amazed by the awesome power of Christ. The Lord has answered my prayer with regard to the auto accident our family experienced. And I am given hope...the miracle of hope...for a new beginning to a relationship with my mother.

I recall conversations with my family, especially during the holidays, of words spoken and unspoken harboring unforgiveness and strife. This kept our family (especially mom and I) from understanding and loving each other. It kept us from having the kind of relationship that Jesus had always wanted for us. It stemmed from holding on to the past, its pain, and unforgiveness.

Jesus spoke about this in (John 20:23 NKJV) **"If you forgive the sins of any they are forgiven; if you retain the sins of any they are retained."** As I walk in obedience to the command that Jesus gave to forgive, I open the door to a freedom that Jesus provides for a renewed faith. At best it can become the start of a new family relationship. I realize though that I can only do my part and that reciprocation may or may not happen on the part of other family members.

LORD
GRANT ME THE SERENITY
TO ACCEPT THE THINGS I CANNOT CHANGE
THE COURAGE TO CHANGE THE THINGS I CAN
AND THE WISDOM TO KNOW THE DIFFERENCE

Somehow I believe that my mother has held on to the painful past of that car accident...harboring unforgiveness. This reflected onto my sister and I, reminding her (my mom) of only the tragedy. Late one summer night in August of 1963, our family was injured in an auto accident. Dad was driving. My sister was asleep in the back seat. I was in the front seat sitting on mom's lap. We were driving home from my aunt's farm. I had recently celebrated my third birthday.

I don't remember the accident itself. I have faint memories of being in the hospital…sitting on dad's lap… grandma feeding me mashed potatoes…a little stuffed giraffe…my sister….(why didn't she wake up?)…stuffed animals everywhere in her room… the nurse painting my nails red…a book about a little girl looking for her shoes…the crib where I slept…how cold it seemed…and how awfully white everything looked around me. I remember how heavy my head felt, covered with bandages.

I sustained lacerations to my face from broken glass of the windshield. The car was broadsided. All of us were injured (cuts, bruises, and broken bones). I remember having a cast on my leg and learning to scoot around with it on.

My sister's injuries were the worst. She sustained broken bones in her legs, a dislocated hip, a skull fracture and brain damage. Because of the brain damage she remained unconscious for several weeks.

As a result of that car accident I remember growing up being teased for the scars that remained on my face. I struggled with that fact. Monster face…they called me. I remember the tears. The emotional scars left a mark far more severe than the physical.

I had plastic surgery on my face, initially. Later on when I was eleven yeas old I had plastic surgery again. My parents took me to a large hospital in Chicago for the second surgery. The scars have faded over the years, but I guess I always wanted that face…that face… without the scars.

OUT OF TRAGEDY...
COMES TRIUMPH...

Sometimes we don't understand things. Maybe we are kept from this. But they happen for a reason. Bad things, tragic things, happen. God uses everything in our lives...everything...for the good.

God revealed to me today something I didn't understand...until today...about that car accident. The scars that I carry on my face and the scars that I carry in my life (emotional and relational wounds) are used by God for the good. Yes, the tragic car accident was, and is still, being used for the good of Christ. For out of tragedy...comes triumph.

I'm reminded now of the numerous times over the course of my life, how Christ has used those scars on my face in many ways to witness of His power. His power is made complete in the scars that He carried because He took everything that day upon Himself. He carried my tears, my wounds, and my scars on that lonely day...that lonely day he died on the cross of Calvary.

He suffered for me...for the tears and the scars I carried from that car accident. He used the power of the cross. He used the power that His blood holds to forgive. So He forgave us and we in turn can forgive others. Through forgiveness...we can really learn...how to love people.

(John 3:16-17 NKJV) For God so loved the world that He gave His only begotten Son, that whoever believes in Him should not perish but have everlasting life. 17 For God did

not send His Son into the world to condemn the world, but that the world through Him might be saved.

Yes, that car accident was used many times for the good of Christ. People would come to me and ask about the scars...on my face...I couldn't hide them. They were there! I would take the opportunity to explain them to complete strangers, acquaintances, and sometimes those I knew my whole life.

They might say "What happened to you? What happened to your face? How did you get those scars?" It was those times God used my scars to witness to the good news of Jesus Christ.

I recall saying "We don't know why things happen sometimes... why we get into car accidents, or why tragic things happen. But God spared us for a reason. We're here to do something. We didn't die in that accident. We were given the opportunity to live."

That's why I believe those scars were there for me. Given the opportunity, I would remind people of God's power through His saving grace, and the angels that camped around us. Those scars remind me of the power of prayer for our family to heal. Those scars remind me of how we need the Master's touch to heal from the wounds that invaded our lives on that tragic night. Many people prayed for our family to heal, not only from the immediate wounds, but also from the emotional wounds of the scars left behind.

It's all about His forgiveness and the power of prayer. Yes, God can use every circumstance of our life, no matter how tragic, for the triumph of Jesus Christ.

SHE'S MY BEST FRIEND...

Waking up this morning, my mind was taken back. I was taken back to time spent with my best friend. Remembering days gone by, I couldn't help myself. Looking back it was a time well spent. Memories of love, laughter, and tears, God can use. If I had a wish, what would it be? Would I wish upon a star? No, I believe it would be a hope for one granted prayer "Lord, grant me this prayer...use these days gone by...these memories of my best friend... for your glory".

I was taken back to the snapshot once again. Captured at her daughter's graduation ceremony, it was a moment in time; a precious moment spent with my girls. It was a milestone in her life and mine. It was something that took me back. I found myself daydreaming... of days that happened. They were days spent, half my life...ago.

I replayed the time, realizing how unbelievably fast time flies. Wow! It's been twenty-eight years. Through the thick and the thin... the hard times and the good...we remained friends, no matter what.

God gave us a lasting friendship, a gift.

Knowing this, God uses circumstances and places...in our lives... and friendships, I'm taken back to nursing school. I was living at home with my parents along with my daughter. She was little. Going through the problems of life...and the stress of trying to get along at home...I remember needing a friend.

Nursing school was very hard, not to mention the fact that my part-time work made it difficult to put it all together. With work, going to school, taking care of my daughter, dealing with issues at home, and trying to get my homework done (which was overwhelming for me) I knew…and I longed for…a friend. It was then that we met.

It wasn't right at the beginning, but as the last year of our training began. For some reason, the Lord brought us together. One of the teaching aspects of school involved the practice of placing IV lines. We had to learn the technique of the IV stick.

Pairs of nursing students were selected. She and I got matched up. And…of course…she stuck me and got it. Then it was my turn. I don't know how many times I tried, but I just couldn't find the vein. Needless to say…it made me feel bad…because I'm sure it hurt. I had come to find out later that she had bad veins. In the course of her life she was labeled a hard stick…meaning even the most versed experts in the field had a difficult time accomplishing the task.

So anyway…we didn't hang out at the beginning of our nurses' training. (Maybe it was the pain of the unsuccessful IV stick… just kidding). It all started in the midst of a snow storm. In a parking area at the college I was walking through the snow, holding my daughter's hand. Struggling with my book bag, I remember sliding all the way to the school. My future friend…was parked… somewhere near me. She saw me…eventually making it herself, to the school. It was then we started talking. It was the birth of a friendship…something new. She lived just around the corner from me. I could walk to her house.

Nearing springtime, I was having some transportation problems. She offered her passenger seat. We started on the path to developing a friendship. We studied together, too.

She was going through a divorce. I helped her with that. She helped me in getting over my loneliness, during breakups with boyfriends. We helped each other during times of struggle. We leaned on each other.

About that same time, she was admitted to the hospital. Even with her illness, she was instructed to do…make up work…for missing scheduled classes. I helped her with her homework. She was assigned to write a term paper…nursing instructors call…a care plan.

Too sick to hold up her head…feverish and weak…her eyes could barely focus. I chuckled this morning as I remember…she got an A on a paper…that I, out of great compassion have to say…truthfully… wrote (getting a B on it myself)…she needed me then.

In all of the circumstances, we started on a road to a long friendship…and have been friends every since. God has used this friendship over time, and helped us…help each other…even though we didn't always agree. We've had our share of ups and downs, but God used that friendship in many ways.

Eventually we both left the area. We couldn't find jobs. We applied for positions at hospitals in different cities. We eventually secured employment, which led us to move away from home. We moved together. She found a place in the outskirts of the city, approximately 100 miles south of home. I found an apartment a few miles away from her…in a smaller community.

We came to understand each other and had a lot of fun. Our kids grew up together. We leaned on each other for a lot of things. Sometimes we'd get boyfriends and not hang out as much…but we always came back to each other in friendship.

Our spirits were kindred…coming back together…as if we had never been apart. We would talk and talk and laugh and laugh. I remember through the struggles of life…it ended up we were there… for each other.

A NEW LIFE

When my oldest daughter was seven, I met a man and eventually got married. Through the course of the marriage, I experienced tremendous heartache. Because of the circumstances, I went to my knees in prayer. My relationship with Christ was strengthened.

I was led to a place in a park near our home. I called it my quiet place. God led me there to pray. I sought the guidance of the Master Counselor…Jesus. Seeking the Lord in my quiet place…I came to know…an abundance of hope.

Jesus was there. He spoke to me several times. I'm reminded of my quiet place…daily…even now. Sometimes I miss it. But I'm in Little Rock, Arkansas, now. I'm trying to find a quiet place here and I think I've found it. It's in a park called Pinnacle Mountain.

Pinnacle Mountain is amazing. But even more amazing is the fact that God has given me the privilege and the opportunity to witness to His majesty. He took me through the valley of sorrow and is leading me up the mountain. Unbelievable my address here is Green Mountain Drive and my quiet place (I think) will be Pinnacle Mountain. Through it all, I look back at the circumstance of meeting my best friend, I'm reminded of the time…she relocated, out of state…down south.

Once relocated in the south, she began a journey. It was a journey of her own life's struggles. We were apart, but remained friends. I went to visit her a number of times.

Visiting her, traveling back and forth, there was an uneasiness...a restlessness. I couldn't shake the feeling...that something wasn't right. My eyes had not been opened. I prayed for enlightenment. I asked God to expose the cause of my uneasiness.

I remember a visit that took place years after she moved. She invited me to visit. I went, (I was there for about a week) where she lived. God opened my eyes and allowed me to see what it was that wasn't right. Through Him, He revealed to me, the problem.

She was involved in a same sex relationship. The knowledge of this brought heartache. My spirit was crushed. I was saddened by the fact that she had hidden the truth.

I felt betrayed. Over time, I know now, she wanted to tell me. Many times we would sit at coffee. She thought about it but couldn't. She believed if I had known I would walk away from our friendship.

After the sin was exposed, I came home and began to pray for her. I gave her the opportunity to say...whatever she could...about what she needed to let me in on...in her life...and she couldn't do it. But I knew. I think now, that probably...she knew...that I knew.

After the visit I began to pray. I began to search for myself, in my own strength, and sometimes...in the strength of the Lord...for answers. I went to my knees in prayer. On my knees, and sometimes prone, I prayed that God would begin to do a work in her. I prayed that He would bring her out of the sin of the lifestyle she was leading. My hope for her was to experience freedom. Freedom from the bondage of the sin she was involved in.

I remember a night of prayer. I poured out my heart to the Lord. I prayed for a sign, that He was going to being a work. I yearned for the day...He would complete it.

A few hours later...I hurriedly drove to work. The drive was along a blacktop road, lined with pumpkin fields. It was early morning. Running late, I came to a familiar stop sign. I waited for the traffic to clear. I remembered last evening's prayer.

As I waited, I saw a spectacular view peeking over the horizon—the sunrise. I thanked God for the view, realizing that being late for work was a blessing in disguise.

I continued to pray as I drove. The drive took me west. I saw the sun rising in my rear view mirror. I prayed…in my heart…Jesus spoke…and said. "I am there with her." He let me know…He was the one. He was going to take care of her. Jesus let me know; I needed to trust Him.

As I drove I saw a mist…a mist of tiny rain drops hitting the windshield of my car. I looked up and saw a rainbow. Seeing the rainbow reminded me of one thing. God was there. He loved her. He let me know I should continue to love her and hold her in prayer.

(Matthew 11:28 NIV) Come to me, all you who are weary and burdened, and I will give you rest.

I was weary. I was burdened. Jesus revealed to me the way…the only way…I could find rest was to lay her at the foot of the cross. It was difficult for me. My personality lends itself to repairing problems. I prayed "Please God, please begin a work in her life". I went to see her once again, years later.

(James 4:8 NKJV) Draw near to God and He will draw near to you.

I remember the visit. She left the lifestyle and moved back home. She thanked me for my prayers. She thanked me for the words I had spoken. God led me to help her come to an understanding. Presently she's married. She let me know God had done a work. Our friendship was meant for a reason.

No, the reason wasn't revealed in the beginning. It wasn't until years later God allowed me to understand His purpose in our friendship. I served the Lord in helping her. He allowed us to continue in close friendship sustained over many years for prayer…

for enlightenment. God's love for her was revealed through a friendship of support through prayer.

It took years to build a closeness. It took a closeness like we had to help me come to an understanding. Nobody is too far gone in their sin …that they can't come out.

Through it all I learned much about God and His fellowship. I learned about His promises, His promise of love. After she came out of the lifestyle, I was given a renewed sense of hope in God's redeeming grace. His redeeming grace can free us from the shackles of sin…that keep us believing the lies of Satan. He can use us to witness to people. He can use us to help others know what they need to do…to draw near to God.

THE TORNADO ...

In keeping with His ways, God uses us through friends and circumstances, being witnesses to His power. He can also use us as instruments through the means of intercessory prayer. There are times people need Christians as prayer warriors to intercede for them.

As followers of Christ, God can bring knowledge of circumstances or people to mind; whether they be acquaintances, family members, friends, or strangers. When we ask God for this knowledge, and He allows us the privilege, it is His desire that we walk in obedience to Him and pray. Restated, if someone comes to mind…pray…for them. I'm learning to trust God in this part of my prayer life.

I'm reminded of another friendship, a bond that grew over a few years during my career. She was also experiencing a troubled marriage. Marriage difficulties were a common factor to both of us. This commonality led me to pray for her. She told me…she prayed for me.

We came to know each other through work. I met her husband as he stopped in to visit her at the center…passing through town. He was a truck driver.

I'm reminded of an event that occurred in the spring.

The weather seemed strange today. It was warm--a bit too warm for this time of year. It was springtime--one of those days you could smell the coming of a storm. The sky was gray. It seemed restlessly calm. I left work earlier than expected. Above, I could see clouds gathering, turning black as the storm approached.

Miracles of HOPE

I started the drive home, praying all the while for my youngest daughter. The nursery school was 15 miles away. I clicked on the radio and heard weather reports. Eventually the roar of emergency sirens whistled in my ears. Tornados had been spotted in several nearby areas.

I rounded the corner a block from home. The wind had picked up. There was outdoor furniture strewn in the neighbor's yard. Hurriedly I scooped up my toddler and two dogs. We headed for the basement. The wind howled outside the basement window casings. The sound of driving rain beat against the panes. Looking out the window, it seemed the trees were bowing down.

I continued to pray for safety. "Jesus…please come…please keep my family safe." The lights were flickering on and off. Suddenly I head the whistle of sirens. The firehouse was a few blocks away. The sirens signaled the town of a tornado spotted in the vicinity.

My daughter was restless. I tried to stay calm as I searched for the TV remote. I wondered. Where were the tornados? I continued in my prayers for the safety of my family.

Overhead lights flickered and then went out. There was enough light from a side window that allowed me to see. I kept searching for the TV remote. I'm not sure why…without electricity…the TV wouldn't work.

As I searched for the remote…I prayed. Then a thought hit my brain. I knew it was from the Lord. The thought was, "pray for Dennis."

I didn't know Dennis. I didn't know who He meant by Dennis. I said out loud "Who's Dennis?" I knew I had to pray for him. A short prayer followed: "Lord…whoever Dennis is…wherever he is… keep him safe…send your angels…watch over him…take care of him." My thoughts returned to my family.

The lights flickered again. Some time later, the electricity stayed on. I found the remote. Relieved, I turned on the TV… channel surfing to find a news station.

I tuned in to the end of a broadcast. The news reporter was stationed somewhere in the city where I worked, near an expressway.

She covered a story about a truck driver who survived a horrendous accident.

The truck was driven into the eye of the tornado. It was stated that the truck was lifted up into the funnel. It was also stated that the driver survived.

I did not see views of the driver. His name was not revealed during the time I viewed the broadcast. Astonished, I found it difficult to imagine that anyone could survive such an event.

All night long I couldn't get the truck accident off my mind. It was the weekend so I was off work. I didn't see or hear anything more about the accident or the truck driver.

(Psalm 46:1 NKJV) God is our refuge and strength, a very present help in trouble.

(Psalm 46:10 NKJV) Be still, and know that I am God.

Monday morning came. I worked the late shift. Arriving at the clinic, I stepped into the break room. It was a busy time on the clinic floor. I wondered "Why are this many people on break simultaneously?"

Walking past a room full of people, I headed for my locker. My friend, Phyllis was standing in the middle of the crowded room. Thoughts of the accident flooded my mind. Opening my locker, I exclaimed "Did you see the broadcast about the truck driver...the one that survived the eye of the tornado?" I gasped. "I can't believe it! I'm amazed! What happened? How could he survive?"

The whole room became silent. You could hear a pin drop. I looked around. Nobody said a word. My friend was standing in the middle of the room. I looked at her. She looked at me. Her eyes filled up with tears. Then she said "Valerie...that was my husband."

I looked at her. All of a sudden I realized her husband's name was Dennis. My eyes filled up with tears. I could barely swallow.

I knew I must tell her what happened. I must tell her my prayer. There were a number of my work colleagues standing and listening. I was in awe as I learned of the miraculous refuge God provided for him. We both hugged…and cried.

I told her about my experience the night of the tornado. I shared about the fact that the Lord had brought a name to my mind. I testified about the fact that I did not realize it was her husband. I repeated my prayer for him, asking God to send His angels…and whoever he was…please keep him safe.

I told her about seeing the end of the news broadcast. I told her no matter how hard I tried…I couldn't get the accident off my mind. She explained her husband had no injuries from the accident. I was awestruck, in awe of the power of God.

A few months later, my friend's husband came into the clinic. He had come to visit. I'm sure she let him know I prayed for him, his safety and protection, the angels, and that God would take care of him.

I saw a big 'ol truck driver guy walk in. He picked me up off my feet, giving me a bear hug. He thanked me for my prayers. He said he should have died in the accident.

I thank God for the opportunity to pray for him, and for the refuge God provided in the midst of his trouble. He placed this person on my mind for prayer. Given these opportunities provided a witness to more people in the break room as they heard the story. I know the testimony was planned. It wasn't an accident.

My entrance into the break room, the timing, and God's presence provided a miracle. Miraculous, wonderful things happen when we pray. The earthly winds of a tornado became a mighty miraculous wind of God.

PINNACLE MOUNTAIN

Today I went to Pinnacle Mountain. Wow! What a climb!
The mountain is located in Little Rock, Arkansas. Drawn to this mountain on a Sunday afternoon, I wanted to take a trail hike. And what a hike it was…at least an hour, before you reach the most difficult aspect of the climb. The climb took over two hours, reaching the top. Boulders and cliffs marked a path that seemed insurmountable at times.

On my way to the starting point, I remember praying. Talking to God at the beginning of the trail, I asked Him to speak to me as I climbed. But there were times I couldn't listen for what He had to say. I had to place my concentration and effort on the path, leading to the top.

In order to keep my footing, I watched for painted markers. Sometimes I couldn't see the markers until I got right on top of them. It was at that point I could see the next marker.

I learned from the climb that I had to focus, concentrating on the path beneath my feet, making sure it was solid. I caught spectacular views through the tree lines. Beautiful as they were, it was difficult to resist those views. However, I found that the sureness of my foothold was secure only in focusing on fixed markers, placed along the path by the experts.

Along the way I paced myself…pacing…breathing…resting…climbing. My muscles were giving out and my brain said "let's give up". I thought… "I've come this far, I can't give up now"!

Breathing hard, I sat on a boulder, resting. Then I heard laughter...the sounds of laughter. It gave me strength. I knew. I was near the top.

Wow! I finally made it. The exhilaration was beyond my imagination. What a view! It took my breath away. It was worth it. It was worth the climb.

Taking in the experience, and the magnificent view that stretched out before me, I sat down, trying to catch my breath. I pulled out my pocket Bible, opening to a familiar verse.

(Isaiah 40:31 NKJV) But those who wait on the Lord shall renew their strength; they shall mount up with wings like eagles, they shall run and not be weary, they shall walk and not faint.

It is one of my favorite passages. I savored the words as I rested. I was less than ten feet from the edge of a cliff at the pinnacle. Moments later a bird landed nearby. I watched in amazement as he was...gigantic. His feathers glistened shiny black in the sunlight. I watched him walk slowly on the rocks at the edge. He stopped. Then he turned his body facing outward on the cliff, hanging onto the edge with huge claws. I gazed upon this bird as he slowly spread his wings. He had a wing span of at least six feet.

Wings outstretched...I noted...he didn't jump off...he didn't flap his wings. He just stood there motionless, as if he were waiting. And then...it happened. I felt a wind, coming out of nowhere. It seemed to come from behind...or maybe...underneath.

Suddenly this huge bird was lifted. He was lifted effortlessly, soaring outward and upward, not moving his wings. He just held them there. The wind came along and carried him. Around and around he soared, allowing only the winds to propel his flight. It was a sight...an experience...I will never forget...at the top.

At the top I was able to see across to other pinnacles. The air was thin. I knew I was sitting within some clouds, seeing clouds just pinnacles away on top of other mountains in the horizon. It was almost like being in an airplane. I looked down and saw valleys and riverbeds…people in their cars…looking very small.

I could see just about everything up there. I realized then, at the top of the mountain, there's not a whole lot of vegetation. It's very dry. I saw very few plants. Most were covered with dead leaves. It's not real green. But in the valley…it is.

When I think back, over the course of my life, to the times I've been in the valley, the valley is a place where God strengthened my relationship with Him, thus revealing the valley to me as a place of abundance. Fertile soil and water abound. Plush vegetation thrives. Through God's work, in my own valley, I experienced growth.

But in the valley is where I experienced sorrow, grief and despair. That's where I had been for many years. My marriage was in the valley and I yearned relentlessly to get to the edge. Somehow I knew that the edge of the mountain was the end of the valley. I prayed that God would allow me to start the climb…the climb to the top.

After experiencing Pinnacle Mountain, I thank God for the opportunity to be there. Most of all, getting to the top, where I could witness the awesomeness of the mountain range. I thank God also, for letting me see the valley. From up there the valley didn't seem quite as long. In the long walk of the valley, prayer took place… prayer that happened at a quiet place in Illinois.

A QUIET PLACE

I had a quiet place in Illinois that was close to my house. I was led to this place after leaving the apartment complex that was once my home for four years. It was during a time in my life that led to marriage. It was a place I went, over the course of 14 years, seeking God's strength for the sorrow I experienced in my marriage. In my prayers today, God has encouraged me to write about my Quiet Place.

In 1995 I recorded a song called, "A Quiet Place." The lyrics to this song best describe what I call my Quiet Place. I was led there to seek God and His help, to listen for His voice, and to pray.

It was there I would go…sometimes…to sit and listen. It was there God strengthened me. Yes, it was there that His presence in this Quiet Place ministered to me…even when words and prayers were too difficult to utter…there was incredible healing.

My Quiet Place was in a wooded area, located at a nearby park. That's exactly what it was…in a park…in the woods. The trees were all encompassing, bringing forth a brilliance of colors with the passing of seasons. It was beautiful. I found strength and hope in the beauty of nature. I went there many times, and many times I would be alone.

Alone…with God…in my Quiet Place, I walked. I walked far enough into the wooded areas of the park to find a quietness and peace. Traffic noise was eluded, and in its place came the sounds of nature. Birds, squirrels, and butterflies, along with whispers of gentle breezes ushered in the splendor…the majesty of God. It was for me…a place of rest…a miracle of hope…a Quiet Place.

It reminded me of how God is the Creator of all nature. It was a place where there was an unfathomable witness to the majesty of God, not only as the Creator of all nature, but also to the fact that he created me. It was a miracle of strength and hope…being born in my heart.

When I first came to my Quiet Place, I found comfort in the quietness of being alone. I remember pulling into the park, turning off the engine, and getting out of my car. I stood within a large clearing.

Sometimes I would walk past the clearing into the woods, coming upon other smaller clearings. In awe of the splendor of God's nature, He spoke about whatever struggle I was facing, and about the sorrow I carried in my marriage. I had questions about a lot of things. I questioned Him about the pain. I didn't understand why I had to go through all of that. And so I would go to this Quiet Place many times, to pray.

I remember one day going there. It was mid-morning, in early autumn. The leaves hadn't quite turned yet. I saw leaves turning yellow, mixed with green. Back through the woods I walked. I heard crunching of leaves. I walked along the tree line that resembled a fence. Over the tree line, I noticed a smaller clearing. It was further into the woods. The light was filtering through the trees.

With my eyes, I followed the light downward until it reached a place. It was a place I had never seen before. To me, it looked like a small sanctuary. I made it my sanctuary. It was a place where God ministered to me, and strengthened me. I went there, to my small sanctuary, seeking Him in prayer. I was quieted. My spirit was refreshed. My hope was renewed in this place of peace.

Over time I can remember discovering new areas of the park. It was a large park that had several trails. I tried to find new places to walk, and look for Him. One day I found a new road. It went farther back near bushes, trees, and hills. It ended at the top of a hill. Just over the top I saw an orchard.

I walked along a path, to the back of the orchard. It was quite a distance. At the end of the orchard was a cemetery.

I spent time looking at epitaphs that were engraved on headstones. I was reminded of one thing. Sometimes we don't know why…why we go through things. I just needed to stay in the valley, at that time, for some reason. I didn't know why.

I stayed in the valley holding my husband up in prayer. Through it all, God strengthened me. His strength was what got me through… even though I didn't understand.

There were times I faced sorrow…like a sword going in and out of my heart. In the midst of the sorrow, Jesus came to me, giving me an incredible sense of joy. Though the sorrow was there, the joy overpowered it. Looking back, I know I needed to learn how to trust Him, but that walk in the valley was long.

And it was long. The weariness of my walk in the valley endured over the length of my marriage, a period of several years. There were times I was taken to the mountain, where I could breathe again, where I could stand at the top, like I did at Pinnacle today. So I could face more of the pain I had to go through for some reason. Now I know, God was working in me, the fact that I could trust Him, in every circumstance, no matter what. The Lord of hope… Jesus…was teaching me to trust Him

His work was making my trust more complete. As I walk the journey this side of heaven, my Quiet Place has become a source of strength…a source of hope. I call it a miracle…a miracle of quiet strength.

Spring

Winter

Autumn

Summer

My grandmother wrote these verses in a Bible she presented to me on my confirmation day.

(Proverbs 3:5-6 NKJV) Trust in the Lord with all your heart, and lean not on your own understanding; 6 in all your ways acknowledge Him, and He shall direct your paths.

I believe these verses were chosen especially for me. Drawing near to Him, these words have become etched in my mind making a difference in my life. Undoubtedly, I have spoken this throughout my life's journey.

THE VALLEY OF THE SHADOW... OF DEATH...

I couldn't understand why the doctors hadn't transferred him to ICU. He was not a candidate for the general urology unit. Night after night the nursing team struggled to take care of him. I knew he needed more than we could give, more intensive monitoring. I prayed at his bedside as I cared for him.

Eventually his case became severe. Physicians hesitated in transferring this man to ICU. I moved the emergency cart into his room. Monitoring his heart rhythm off the crash cart, in my heart I prayed "Jesus help him...please help him".

He was deathly ill. The shadow of death was upon him. I had seen it before. There was an instant when he spoke, "I can see Jesus coming down the road...please pray for me. I'm ready, but I have two kids and a wife at home."

Tears falling, I held his hand. I prayed for his recovery. In my heart I knew if Jesus was coming to take him home, it was this man's time to be with the Lord. A few minutes later the crash cart that was already in his room was used. Code blue...code blue...I performed CPR, as the life was snuffed from his body.

He was transferred immediately to ICU. Yes, he lived. His case was considered grave. I held his hand and prayed as we rushed to the intensive care unit, not sure of what the future would hold for this man and his family.

Urology/nephrology was the floor where I took charge duties. It was a hospital known for its wealth of healing to this type of patient.

I still wondered at the time "Why hadn't he gotten moved sooner to the intensive care unit? What were the doctors waiting for? Maybe his chances would have been better had he been moved sooner." Still, Jesus…the miracle of hope…was there.

It didn't bother me if my fellow nurses teased me for my faith. I spoke boldly about Jesus. Those working alongside knew that I was a Christian.

The bed was made ready for another patient. The experience of that night lingered in my thoughts. Time passed.

I transferred to a specialty unit within the hospital, called dialysis. I worked within the hospital setting until my youngest daughter was born. After her birth, I began working for an outpatient dialysis clinic.

(Psalm 23:4 NKJV) Yea, though I walk through the valley of the shadow of death, I will fear no evil; for you are with me; your rod and your staff, they comfort me.

(Psalm 27:13-14 NIV) 13 I remain confident of this; I will see the goodness of the Lord in the land of the living. 14 Wait for the Lord; be strong and take heart and wait for the Lord.

It was a busy night--rounds, medications, and paperwork to be done. I paced myself to finish by closing time. The dialysis stations were full tonight. One station was being prepared for someone new.

He relocated here from up north. I sensed that he was nervous. A clipboard of paperwork in hand, I approached the station where he sat.

We talked before I started on paperwork. As I introduced myself, his eyes searched mine…it was as if we had met before that night.

The rest of the evening, I could tell he was still trying to figure it out.

Where had he seen me before? Had we met sometime in the past?

I didn't remember him.

Nothing out of the ordinary happened. Treatment times were ending. Patients were dismissed. I heard him say, "Now I know. Now I know…it's your voice. I remember now. The night Jesus was coming down the road, I was sick in the hospital. You prayed for me. I heard your voice…thank you…thank you for your prayers."

My heart was bursting. I told him the credit belongs to God. We hugged. It was a miracle! It was a miracle…of hope.

I counted back to the time I worked in the hospital…to the night when I saw him last. At least ten years had passed. Thank you God… for the things you have done for me, and for that man. Thank you, Jesus, for your miracle of hope.

DAUGHTER'S WORDS

I remember something my youngest daughter said to me, when she was seven years old…

"Mommy…you know what?"

What?

Her reply, "There are three ways God answers our prayers. He says yes, no, or wait."

Out of the mouth of a child, comes a profound statement.

I have recited this conversation along the journey of my life. Thank you God for my youngest daughter. I call her a beacon of light in a darkened world.

THE CHRISTMAS MIRACLE...

She was a woman of tall stature, big boned, with broad shoulders. She introduced herself with a whisper. Her husband saddened as he told me she had lost her voice after having surgery for a broken ankle. She was an opera singer.

I related to this well. I remember having trouble with my own voice after undergoing anesthesia. I had surgery to remove the hardware after an ankle fracture. No words could comfort her. She whispered, "I've given up. I have no hope."

She came across my path, having lost her kidney function, needing dialysis. A broken ankle resulted in a near death experience as she was dismissed from the hospital. She had fallen at home and stayed a few days in the hospital to recover. It was a simple surgery to repair a broken bone.

She explained that she was on the hospital elevator, after discharge and fell unconscious after feeling a sharp pain in her side. A heart surgeon happened to be riding the same elevator. He recognized the symptoms and rushed her to surgery, saving her life. It was a moving blood clot that became lodged in her lungs. The odds of surviving such an incident are very low.

Later on she had difficulty walking due to leg pain and wore a brace. Her voice was a whisper as she tried to explain her vocal cords were damaged. She wasn't dealing well with her loss of kidney function. She cried. She let me know she couldn't go on, not like this. She expressed the possibility of stopping treatments.

Depression had fallen upon her. Her husband revealed they had stopped going to church. I didn't know what to say. I told her I would keep her in my prayers. So I did. I prayed.

A few weeks went by. I could tell she was starting to trust me. It takes new patients a while to build trust in those caring for them. I encouraged both to pray and to seek the Lord in the depression and illness. Still in my prayers I remember praying for some relief... please Lord...a healing. If not a healing, then help them to come to know you better through all of this.

I remember telling her not to give up hope, and to keep praying for His peace through all of this. I knew I couldn't give her false hope of a healing for her kidneys...but at the same time...I believed. I did! I told her that. I told her...I believe in miracles...the miracle of hope...Jesus.

It was the night before Christmas Eve. As she left that night to go home, she and her husband told me they had started back to church and had begun praying together. I was elated. She asked me to pray. She asked me to pray for a miracle for her. Of course I would. I promised I would stop at the church that night...to pray for God's will. If it be His will...she would fully recover from her kidney failure...and most of all sing again.

I remember hearing my own footsteps echo, as I entered the foyer of the church. I kept my promise. I knelt at the altar. In the darkness, I could see the Christ candle hanging, next to the pulpit, with the flicker of a flame through red tinted glass. I asked for a full recovery and most of all, that she would come to know Jesus. I expected a miracle. Please Lord, give her a miracle of hope.

It was a simple prayer. I left for home, exhausted from work and all the holiday hubbub. I fell into bed and smiled to know; though I wasn't close to being ready for Christmas, I had stopped to pray. I fell asleep believing a miracle...a miracle of hope at Christmastime...Jesus.

It was the day after Christmas. I had spent the last two days decking the halls, shopping the malls, packing and wrapping to the sounds of Christmas music. I was glad to know the Christmas rush was over.

Presents, wrapping, and rush…rush…rush…seem to fade the sparkle of Christmas. A babe, born in a manger, the true meaning of it all, is left behind far too often. Still, amongst the sheep and the cows, the kings and the shepherds, the miracle of hope was born.

Christmas Eve candlelight service was packed. It was standing room only. I wish every service was like that. I thought about the simple prayer less than 24 hours ago…right here in the sanctuary. I watched candles flickering, and faces lit up as we sang Silent Night. I hoped and prayed the opera singer was celebrating Jesus' birth as well.

Now, with Christmas rush over, it was time to go back to work. What a relief! I worked the late shift. Driving to work, I thought about the opera singer. This was her night for a treatment…I knew I would be seeing her. I couldn't wait to find out how her holiday went!

The minute I saw her, I knew something was different. Her face glowed. I could see sparkle in her eyes. "What happened?" I said.

"I've been healed. I was lying in bed on the night before Christmas Eve. I prayed and prayed. I wanted a miracle. I prayed for a healing. Suddenly a light came in through the bedroom window. It hit my body…and I got a warm feeling all over. It was peaceful. I wasn't afraid. A few minutes later I started urinating. My kidneys… my kidneys…I'm healed!"

No longer needing dialysis…I saw her a year later. The woman… the opera singer…was singing again! Her leg brace was gone. There were no traces of a limp. She brought me a tin filled with Christmas cookies. There was a card on top…thanking me for my prayers.

I still believe. I believe in miracles! Most of all, the miracle of hope…Jesus…that gave the opera singer a glimmer of Himself…at Christmastime.

LIKE POOLS OF BLUE WATER...

He weighed less than 16 pounds. His mother hung desperately to my arm as I approached the critical care unit. I could hear the sobbing of his father outside the room. They were heart-wrenching sobs that moved my heart, so to speak, beyond words.

There was nothing you could say, nothing you could do, except remain calm. Inside I cried for this little one, tears held back in an effort to soothe his mother.

This little one had sustained an emergency helicopter lift from a small hospital up north. His life hung in the balance. At midnight I picked up the phone to hear the doctor say "We have a lot of work to do." I had just finished an 18-hour shift. I was exhausted and itching to go home.

My job required being on call, so the case was mine. I scrambled to find any information I could to help this little one. Unable to find information, I telephoned a veteran nursing peer. She said, "I've never done the procedure. I don't believe it's been done at this hospital." Hanging up the phone, I began to pray.

In a cradle, the baby, this little one, lay limp. The medication and equipment was staggering to see. A team of physicians and nurses did everything they could to keep him alive until the procedure he needed was ready.

A small room two floors below was the preparation room for the machine. An order was telephoned for a specialty item...a special blood line. Intensive care didn't have it. We didn't have it.

"Lord, help me find this tube" I prayed. It was the graveyard shift. I found it hard to believe the supply clerks would have any idea where to get this specialty item. Maybe on the day shift there might be a chance, I thought.

I telephoned central supply. I heard their reply, "What did you say? What did you say you needed?" I repeated the name of the specialty item, praying all the while for the Lord's intervention.

It was a miracle! The supply clerk said they decided to clean some of the bins in the back room. She happened to have the item in her hand as we were speaking.

The treatment made ready for the baby…came natural to me…as if I had done it before. I knew that Jesus was there…the miracle of hope.

He hadn't cried in a long time. His eyes were closed. His body was wasting away from the virus. Blond hair found in his cradle, falling out. The virus threatened his life. I wondered, "Could he be saved?" I prayed.

I remember how intense the air felt as I entered his room. His mother cried down the hallway. "Save my baby…save my baby" I heard. In my heart I prayed "Lord don't leave us…we need you!"

Minutes in that room…twenty-five minutes…that's all it took from start to finish. It was complete. We had done our part.

I stood at his bedside, my eyes intently watching. I was looking for signs, signs of new movement. I could see his long eyelashes. His eyes were shut. The room was silent except for the sounds of machines. It was as if everyone in the room was holding their breath. All of us watched as this little one lay in his cradle. Suddenly, like pools of blue water, his eyes looked straight at mine. He cried! Yes, he cried!

It was the most glorious sound I had heard in a long time! Praise the Lord! I heard from the physician years later that he had grown and he was healthy. Jesus, the miracle of hope, was there for him. I'll never forget that night. Yes, I believe! Prayer changes things. Jesus gave this little one the miracle of life.

FROM HELL TO HEAVEN ...

Working at the clinic that day was one of the more challenging days I had in a long time. Today was what I called blood day. I had several units of blood to hand. It was transfusions galore.

I double-checked paperwork on the transfusions and noted the time. Looking at the clock, I prepared for the afternoon shift. The unit was being cleaned and prepped for the next set of patients.

The parking lot in front of the clinic was busy. Vans, buses, and cars were coming and going. Patients came in and out of the clinic. The telephone rang constantly. (Grand Central Station, I thought.). The list of duties seemed endless. Focusing on the task at hand, I stood at the front desk. It was then I heard a cry. It was a cry for help. Voices shouted and I heard, "Call 911, she's dead." I ran toward the sound of the cry. The bus driver was frantic.

Maxine was grumpy. I rarely saw her smile. It seemed she carried a sadness. I sensed something surrounded her, like an invisible cloak. Was it a cover of loneliness? Her assigned station was behind glass, in a small isolated room. She was secluded from the other patients because of her condition. I rarely saw her family. She lived in a room at a nearby nursing home. It could have been her apparent disposition stemmed from her loneliness.

Maxine has been a patient at the clinic for some time. Since I first met her, she aged a lot beyond her years. Her eyes seemed to tell the story of her life, of her loneliness. For some reason I took a liking to Maxine. On the days she was there, I recited stories and poems. In an effort to cheer her, there were times I shared photos and family stories. I wanted to bring some laughter into her life. I hoped to see her smile.

But Maxine didn't smile very often. I recall one day she asked a question. She said, "Why do you take a liking to me? What is it that makes you different from everyone else?" It was then I shared the age-old story of Jesus. I told her it didn't matter--her grumpy disposition. She explained to me several times that she did not believe in God. In her grumpy way she told me, "I'm an atheist."

It was Maxine, the grumpy, lonely, woman we laid on the pavement. Outside the clinic door, kneeling beside her, we called 911. Doing CPR we tried our best to bring life back to Maxine. She was frigid and cold, her color blue. Lifting her out of the wheelchair, I remember her body remained positioned as if she was still seated.

Sometime during the bus ride to the clinic, Maxine and the life she knew was snatched away. Fellow workers rushed to care for her. Emergency equipment was brought to her side. It seemed hopeless at the time. Was it too late?

For an instant, I thought about the times she said, "I don't believe in God. No, there is no God. Jesus doesn't exist."

In my mind and in my heart I began to pray. "Jesus come. Jesus please come. Jesus, please come now! She said you're not real. She said she didn't believe in you. Please forgive her! Jesus, please forgive Maxine!"

I don't know whether it was the moment, or the adrenaline flow of the emergency; or Christ's presence as we knelt beside her. But one thing I do know. He was there! Jesus, the miracle of hope, was there. His power and strength surged through me.

(Philippians 4:13 NKJV) I can do all things through Christ who strengthens me.

At that moment it didn't matter whether my fellow nurses heard my plea for Christ's mercy. So I began to pray out loud. "Maxine… Maxine…come back! You are not dead…you're alive! You are…you are coming back to life! It's not your time to die. Please Maxine… please Jesus…help us…Jesus help her!"

I began to recite The Lord's prayer.

Our Father
Who art in heaven
Hallowed be thy name
Thy kingdom come
Thy will be done
On earth as it is in heaven
Give us this day our daily bread
And forgive us our debts
As we forgive our debtors
And lead us not into temptation
But deliver us from evil
For thine….

Finally, in the midst of the crisis…she took a breath. Yes, she came back! She was alive. The ambulance came and paramedics rushed her to the hospital.

Over the next few days, I thought about Maxine. I prayed for her. I prayed for God's comfort and peace. I thanked God for giving her a second chance.

Upon returning to work a few days later my assignment was unusual. I hadn't been to the main hospital for quite some time. I was assigned to go to ICU to care for Maxine.

Entering her room, I looked at her. Maxine was asleep. Even when her eyes were open, she wasn't there. She was gone. It was inevitable. The time frame with no oxygen to her brain and vital organs, on the bus ride, had left Maxine asleep, even in her waking moments.

I talked to her as I worked. I hoped she could hear me. Nearing the end of my time with her, the family came to her bedside. They thanked me for my time in caring for her. Her daughters thanked me for being there the day we called 911. We spoke briefly about Maxine's belief. Her family confirmed her statements that she said she was an atheist. My heart sank. Her daughter explained about the times she tried to help her mother find Christ.

I was saddened today at her bedside. We held hands and prayed for Maxine. In my heart, I hoped she would have a second chance. Would you Lord? Could you Lord? Give her a miracle, a second chance, I thought.

I was standing at the end of her bed. Suddenly, without warning, Maxine raised her hand and pointed her finger straight at me. I swallowed hard. For a moment, it felt as if my blood ran out of my head and straight to my feet. It was as if I was witnessing a death to life experience.

She said, "You're the one…I heard your voice…you're not dead… you're alive…you're coming back to life…it's not your time to die… please Jesus." She told us then how she saw the fire…the gates…the demons…felt the cold…and saw the awful darkness of that place. She cried as she explained how she heard someone praying… "Our Father…who art in heaven…hallowed be thy name." She said at that moment her body started floating backwards. She said she saw that awful place, as she floated backwards from the coldness. She said she went upwards toward the sound of the voice praying.

My eyes filled with tears. To this day, I stand amazed. I stand in awe of God.

Later on I heard from her family. Maxine passed away. She passed away not long after the day I last saw her. Before her death she called for a pastor, confessed her sin, and gave her heart to Christ.

Wow! What a difference we can make in someone's life if we only take time to pray…to believe…if we take time to believe in the miracle of hope…Jesus.

I believe in the miracle. I believe in Him. I believe in His power.

I believe in Christ! Yes, I believe!

UNFORGETABLE ...

It was the fall of 1996--September 20th, to be exact. On this sunny autumn day, a child was born...my first grandchild. I call him a miracle...a miracle boy.

From the time of his birth, I couldn't take my eyes off him. His little face was adorable. Everywhere we went, people said "Isn't he cute! What a cute baby!"

I remember the day...the weekend...when she gave me the news. I didn't take it too well. Looking back, I wish that I would have handled it better. She was too young...I thought. She was too young to become a mother.

I guess I felt confused, or maybe I had my own ideas of how my daughter's life should unfold. To some extent, I know most parents share the same considerations on the part of their children.

After getting over the shock of the news, I was anxious for my daughter. I prayed. I prayed for my daughter and her future. I prayed for my grandchild, for his health, and for their future together.

The whole experience of her pregnancy and the first few months of his life were an answer to prayer. I was proud of the fact that my daughter decided to continue her education...even in the midst of her pregnancy. I knew that Jesus...the miracle of hope... was there. What courage it must have taken to walk the halls of the high school, knowing all the while a little body was growing and developing inside.

I'm reminded of a story in Luke:

(Luke 8:22-25 NCV) 22 One day Jesus and his followers got into a boat, and he said to them "Let's go across the lake." And so they started across. 23 While they were sailing, Jesus fell asleep. A very strong wind blew up on the lake, causing the boat to fill with water, and they were in danger. 24 The followers went to Jesus and woke him, saying "Master! Master! We will drown!" Jesus got up and gave a command to the wind and the waves. They stopped and it became calm. 25 Jesus said to his followers "Where is your faith?" The followers were afraid and amazed and said to each other, "Who is this that commands even the wind and the water, and they obey him?"

It took me back to my own experience, learning to cope with pregnancy at a young age. Yes, Jesus was faithful, a faithful friend. Over the next few months, the problems we experienced as a family helped us to grow. The relationship I had with my daughter was changing for the better, in an effort to overcome the hardships we were now facing.

The changes were an answer to prayer. Time passed. The stress and tension somewhat eased. I found…how tickled I was to become a grandmother. I couldn't wait for this little one to be born.

By the time my daughter graduated from high school, my grandson was 9 months old. The first few months of his life were courageous for him…and for his mother.

A few days after his birth, my daughter discovered a bump on the back of his head. Not sure what it was, we made an appointment for him to see a doctor. Within a week he was scheduled for a checkup. His checkup was fine with the exception of this little bump. The doctor thought maybe it was something insignificant… possibly a cyst that could wait to be removed when he was older. For the sake of his health, and to be sure that it wasn't more serious, it was decided he should be examined right away by a specialist.

I remember the anxiety...the nervousness we felt, walking into the doctor's office. It was the office of a specialist, a pediatric neurosurgeon. It seemed at times overwhelming. We wondered.

A brain scan was done. What exactly was this thing? This little bump...what could it be? I prayed. His mother prayed. Our whole family prayed. Tests showed it was a small cyst, held in the skin, on the back of his head.

She was instructed to watch for leakage of fluid from this little bump. The possibility that any leakage was seen could mean that his condition was serious. Fluid was a sign—a sign that the cyst, or whatever it was, could be a tumor inside his brain.

Prayer followed. My daughter and I took this little one into our arms. We surrendered his future and his condition into the arms of the Lord. Kneeling down, we prayed for a miracle...a miracle of healing.

Later on I was awakened in the night by a voice calling my name. I heard my name called three times. After the third time, I knew it was the Lord. I began to pray for my grandson. I heard the Lord speaking to my heart "Do the best you can, and let me handle the rest."

Two weeks later, Kyle had a crying spell that was alarming. His cries were piercing. His mother was unable to comfort him. Then she noticed a tuft of hair that was unusual, growing over the little bump. From this tuft of hair she noticed fluid leaking.

The next month my grandson went through a lot. Between the doctor visits and brain scans (though they showed a cyst that was held under the skin), it was decided he have exploratory surgery. It was at the children's hospital, thirty minutes away, this fragile little life underwent a full day of surgery.

Oh how my heart ached for him. The nervous tension and anxiety I had could only be a fraction of what my daughter carried. Still, what I saw in her was strength. What I saw in her was courage.

(Psalms 111:1-4 NCV) 1 I will thank the Lord with all my heart in the meeting of his good people. 2 The Lord does great things; those who enjoy them seek them. 3 What he does is glorious and splendid, and his goodness continues forever. 4 His miracles are unforgettable.

The pastor arrived in the waiting room. We held hands and prayed. I left the waiting room several times…pacing…meditating, and praying. "Jesus be there" I prayed. "Jesus please be in that room. Jesus be the hands, the eyes, and the mind of the surgeon, as he works to remove the tumor."

I tried to focus on the newspaper. Maybe I'll read. Maybe it would take the edge off the stress, I thought. At this point the newspaper was just a bunch of printed words. The news of the world around me faded in comparison to what my grandson was facing. Fighting tears, behind the guise of the newspaper, I continued to pray.

My thoughts were again taken to the room, the room where he lay on the operating table. Suddenly I felt a sense of peace. The words I heard a few nights before came once again. "Do the best you can. Let me handle the rest."

There was tranquility. In my heart I knew…Jesus…the miracle of hope…was there. I felt assured. Not only was Jesus here with us in the waiting area, but present in the operating room as well. After hours of waiting we learned that he was out of surgery and was moved. We left the waiting area, hoping to see him.

ICU was something I was accustomed to…or so I thought. I had worked there. I had taken care of many patients within these walls. But somehow, it wasn't the same…seeing my grandson lying there… helpless…innocent. My mind raced. It became cluttered with images that petrified…the reality of the moment. I had to remain constant for my daughter. I had to stay calm. Inside, I cried. I wept for the grace…the healing…the mercy of Christ…for my grandson.

The next few weeks were somewhat of a roller coaster. He had high fevers caused by an infection and swollen brain tissue. We found later that a patch had become loosened on his brain. This allowed fluid to leak slowly causing his head to swell to the size of a small pumpkin. His throat swelled to the point of difficulty breathing. He underwent procedures that seemed…at times endless…in his recovery.

Through it all, Jesus…the miracle of hope…was there. My grandson, released from the hospital, began his new little life without the tumor…at home.

The day came for him to see the surgeon for the sutures to be removed. I didn't believe that the skin was ready for this. I told my daughter. She took him to see the doctor. I was scheduled to work. The next thing I know, I'm entering the emergency room hearing the cries of a child just inside one of the exam rooms. I knew that cry. It was my grandson.

He was then rushed to emergency surgery. The sutures had been the only thing holding the loosened patch in place. We were told there was little to no fluid left to send a sample…his spinal fluid gushed out when the sutures were removed. His scalp came open and his brain was exposed. So he was rushed that afternoon to the table… surgery underway. Once again this little life underwent another hospitalization, this one being even more complicated than the first.

My daughter remained strong. I couldn't believe the sense of urgency, boldness, and forthrightness she displayed, as she spoke with the doctor about her son.

God was within our midst. He remained on the throne. Even though it seemed we were falling apart, Jesus remained faithful… our faithful friend.

A few weeks later, released from the hospital, my grandson began his journey at home without the tumor. My grandson, at the age of two months, had climbed a mountain. I should say…Jesus climbed it for him. It was understood, when he was discharged, that he should undergo future testing. This was to be done to detect any abnormal growths.

(Psalms 111:4-9 NCV) 4 His miracles are unforgettable. The Lord is kind and merciful. 5 He gives food to those who fear him. He remembers his agreement forever. 6 He has shown his people his power when he gave them the lands of other nations. 7 Everything he does is good and fair; all his orders can be trusted. 8 They will continue forever. They were made true and right. 9 He sets his people free. He made his agreement everlasting. He is holy and wonderful.

Life continued for my grandson. We watched for signs...there were no signs. He loved school, reading, horses, and most of all, his new baby brother. He continued to have testing done with each one coming back negative...until...one spring day. He was ten years old. Coming home from school, he noticed a bump on the back of his head. It was in the same place as it had been when he was a baby. The bump felt hard.

He saw a doctor. Since the time of his surgery, my daughter and her family had moved out of state. So his new doctor was unfamiliar with his case. My daughter's prompts and probing questions finally led to a decision for a test. They tested the fluid that came from the bump.

Another opinion...an ordered scan...symptoms of a headache...waiting for the day of the test—it seemed too much to bear. Still, Jesus...the miracle of hope...was there.

Off to a major research center they went. Research specialists decided to follow his case. The appointment was set for six months later, a scan showed a mass. This mass was different. It wasn't in the same place. It was inside the skull bone, near his ear...and could cause hearing loss. He was told that it could paralyze the muscles in his face, destroy his skull bones, and could lead to a condition that causes swelling of the brain. Eventually, the mass was given a name.

They weren't quite sure what to do. All we could do was wait. Waiting was difficult. During the wait we prayed and prayed. We sought the Master Physician.

After church one afternoon, my grandson and his family stayed for special prayers. Prayers were lifted up in his behalf. He was anointed with oil. One prayer in particular was a prayer for a miracle…a miracle of healing.

The day arrived—the day of the test. It was spring 2008. Yes, it was one year from the time it was discovered, coming home from school.

Research doctors studied the scan. He waited. His mom waited. They watched the doctors study the films…searching…searching…searching. Five minutes went by. The images of his brain were studied. My daughter watched as different angles of her son's test were scrutinized by the doctors. Anxious, his mother wasn't sure. Was this good news?

Breaking the ice, she said "Well, where is it?" Still there was silence. They continued to search. My daughter walked over, standing behind the doctor himself. The doctor finally stopped searching and said, "I can't find it." "That's what we prayed for," she said.

She heard a quiet chuckle from the doctors. But it wasn't quiet chuckles that came when the rest of the family heard the news. It brought laughter, smiles, tears of joy, and overwhelming praise.

Thank you, Lord, for your miracle of healing. Thank you, Lord, for your miracle of hope. I can't say enough. I just can't say enough.

It was unforgettable.

www.ingramcontent.com/pod-product-compliance
Lightning Source LLC
LaVergne TN
LVHW041550070526
838199LV00046B/1894